Andrew Greeley's Chicago

Andrew M. Greeley

With 175 Photographs by the Author

CONTEMPORARY
BOOKS
CHICAGO · NEW YORK

Library of Congress Cataloging-in-Publication Data

Greeley, Andrew M., 1928–
    [Chicago]
    Andrew Greeley's Chicago / Andrew M. Greeley.
        p.   cm.
    ISBN 0-8092-4440-3
    1. Chicago (Ill.)—Social life and customs.   2. Chicago (Ill.)—
Descriptions—1981–   —Views.   I. Title.
    F548.52.G736   1989
    977.3′11—dc20   89-17437
                                                              CIP

Published by Contemporary Books, Inc.
180 North Michigan Avenue, Chicago, Illinois 60601
Manufactured in the United States of America
International Standard Book Number: 0-8092-4440-3

Published simultaneously in Canada by Beaverbooks, Ltd.
195 Allstate Parkway, Valleywood Business Park
Markham, Ontario L3R 4T8 Canada

Contents

For my neighbors—Maggie, Rich, Nora, Patrick, Lally

"A city set on a mountain top cannot be hidden."

—Matthew 5:14

In Chicago our God lurks everywhere—
In the elevated train's husky roar,
Beside the blinking lights of intensive care,
In the clamor of the soybean trading floor,
With those who suffer poverty and fright,
In the humid mists of summer by the lake,
On the Ryan through an icy winter night,
With a young widow weeping at a wake.

A city of beauty, hilarity, and pain,
Boundless energy and permanent unrest.
A terrifying, troubled, hopeful place—
Its challenges intricate and arcane,
Its opportunity . . . ah, the very best:
To be an unclouded light of love and grace!

Acknowledgments

I want to thank June Rosner for suggesting the tour that led to this book, Nat Sobel for nudging me into doing it, Bernard Shir-Cliff for agreeing to the project, and Georgene Sainati for her advice in selection and layout of the photographs.

I
The City as Sacrament

When she was teaching me self-hypnotism, Erika Fromm once sent me to heaven—lifted up on a beach blanket by four angels. In my altered state, the angels and I strode first of all through a wooded area, which in retrospect was very much like the Thatcher Woods Forest Preserve (the only quasi forest I know). It had to be heaven because I was singing, something that I do not do in this life. We were wearing lincoln green like Robin Hood and his Merry Men (I have no idea why), and the songs were marching melodies, not hymns.

Then we turned a corner in the woods and there was heaven; there were no walls and no ivory-and-gold palaces. Rather, heaven was a great, busy city on the shores of a vast lake; boats cut through the waters of the lake, and planes circled the high towers of the city.

Even in my altered state, there wasn't much doubt what the city was. The heavenly city was a spruced-up Chicago.

For someone raised in the Catholic imaginative tradition, a city is a sacrament, a hint, however flawed and imperfect, of what God is like. In the Catholic sensibility, God lurks in the streets and the buildings, the parks and the neighborhoods, the sights and the sounds of the city.

A Catholic imagines this way in his preconscious because in the Catholic religious sensibility the world is a metaphor for God. A city cannot be evil, though it may have much evil in it. The presence of God in the city is a challenge to make it a more human and humane place.

My friend Harvey Cox, a professor at Harvard Divinity School, discovered first that the secular city is a place of merit in itself. Later he discovered that it is also a revelation of the sacred. Harvey's sensibility has through the years become more and more Catholic. I do not expect those who are in other religious traditions to accept the Catholic notion of the city as sacrament. I merely expect them to try to understand that it is consistent with the underlying Catholic conviction that grace is everywhere.

Hence the revelatory experience that overwhelms Redmond Peter Kane on the banks of the Chicago River in the shadow of the 333 Wacker Building is but one manifestation of my imagination's stubborn conviction that God's self-disclosure is going on all the time in this city.

I do not deny the ugliness—slums, housing projects, gangs, drugs, poverty, corruption. Rather, I say that the Catholic image of Chicago as sacrament demands that the ugliness be purged so that the city becomes a more adequate metaphor for God.

My assignment for this book was to try to create pictures of the world in which the characters of my novels live. Hence my view of the sacramentality of the city is limited to some of the images that my characters are likely to see in their daily life. It is a limited, incomplete, and highly personal view of the city. The images are not a random sample of possible images of Chicago nor even of possible images of the Chicago in my stories. Rather, they are the result of instinctive reactions to the environment in which my characters move—an environment that for all its imperfections is permeated with grace.

II
Sights and Sounds of a City

Chicago, like all cities, is a noisy place. Its citizens scream at each other all day and all night as they strive desperately to gain attention for what they are doing or what they are selling.

At night the wail of an ambulance tells perhaps of a frenzied attempt to save a life; the fire siren warns of an effort to fight the sort of disasters that destroyed great cities in the past, even this one not so long ago; the police alarm describes the never-won battle against crime; the drone of a jet engine hints at the world invading the city and the city opening itself up to the world.

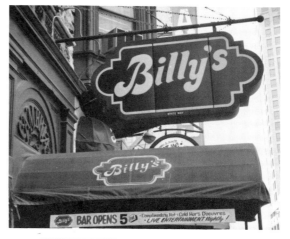

The clang of the telephone jars us from our sleep with good news or bad news or more likely a wrong number. When we cannot sleep we turn on the radio and are soothed by music soft or loud.

The alarm wakes us up with the news that the demands of another day of urban living must be met.

We come in time to hate the noise, even if we cannot live without it and even if we reflect on how essential much of it is and even if we comprehend that God is disclosing Herself in the sounds and the sights of the city.

The signs are visual sounds, persistent and insistent demands that we notice what those who have put up the signs are about—pizza parlors and museums, theaters and video shops, boutiques and Jesuit provincial houses, churches and lingerie shops, elegant restaurants and fast-food emporia, concert halls and drugstores, copying facilities and bakeries.

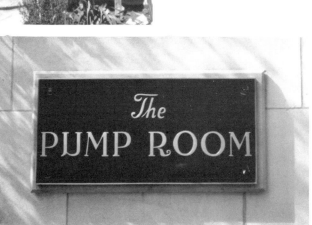

Normally we record and process these signs at the periphery of our consciousness. The characters in my stories stroll down Clark Street or the Magnificent Mile with only the faintest awareness of what the signs are saying. There are so many signs that we hardly notice any of them—unless we are looking for one. Yet we remember a sign later when we are thinking about purchasing goods or a service that the sign offers. Such was the case of poor Brendan Ryan, a quiet man, on a day in May when he walked down Michigan Avenue. He searched for the sign of Dufficy's Irish Store (a creature of my imagination) next to the sign of Stuart Brent's bookstore (which exists in God's world as well as mine). He found adventure and romance that he would not have dreamed possible before that sign caught his eye.

I had entered Dufficy's Irish Store on Michigan Avenue to buy a present for my daughter, Jean, a student at Stanford, who was going to Ireland for the summer.

The woman and I had exchanged a few words, a couple of quickly averted glances. I could hardly remember what she looked like when I stumbled out of the store.

Yet she was my destiny. I knew it. So, it seemed, did she.

The image of her body, pliant and happy under mine, hit me as I was leaving the store. I must have her. I, Brendan Ryan, the quietest of quiet men, had made up his mind.

I must have her. I would have her.

Soon.

Thus spring came violently to Michigan Avenue the last week in April, and with it the beginning of my fall from grace.

I leaned against the window of Stuart Brent's bookstore as exhausted as though I had run four miles. The gentle touch of a morning breeze against my face hinted at the caress of a woman's hand. The delicious lethargy that pervaded my body suggested that I had been enfolded in her embrace, her breasts pressed soothingly against my chest. My lightweight gray suit, prudently withdrawn from mothballs after I had heard the morning weather forecast on WFMT, was already wilted. My tailor-made broadcloth shirt was soaked with sweat.

What did she look like? I must remember. A smile, a soft voice with a touch of the brogue, a white dress, a delicate and tasteful scent . . . nothing more: the beginning, perhaps, of Brendan Ryan's foolish pursuit of the Holy Grail.

—*from* Rite of Spring

III

The Lake and the River

Chicago is the result of several caprices of nature. It is spread across a continental divide that is mostly swamp. Listen to Blackie Ryan describe the origins of the lake as he ponders Monroe Street Harbor from Northly Island, where the 1933 World's Fair was based.

On the way back to the cathedral and chaos, I turned off Lake Shore Drive to Northly Island, site of the 1933 fair and now of Meigs Field and the Adler Planetarium. Having cleansed the city of pollution, the thunderstorm had departed to the eastern horizon. The skyline glowed, spanking clean.

Lake Michigan was, I reflected, one of Lady Wisdom's playful tricks. Twenty-five thousand years ago, the Michigan Basin had been a vast area of wooded lowlands, drained by a complex river system. Then the Wisconsin glaciation had pushed its way south with massive glaciers, including one ten thousand feet high that for some ten thousand years occupied the space where Northly Island and everything else in the area now lay. Then the glaciers melted, forming first Lake Chicago and then, some twelve thousand years ago, Lake Michigan, 923 feet deep, 579 of those feet above sea level.

It made for cooling lake breezes in the summertime.

—*from* Happy Are Those Who Thirst for Justice

We anchored opposite Mies's legendary 900 North Lake Shore Drive apartments ("Less is a bore!" Caitlin had dismissed the famous architect's functionalism) and dove into the placid waters. We swam around the boat till we were exhausted, climbed back in, finished off the salami, and drank the last of the Diet Cokes. Behind us the skyline, presided over by the slender mass of the John Hancock Center, shimmered in humid pastel mists, a light-drenched Impressionist painting.

—*from* Happy Are Those Who Thirst for Justice

Left to itself, the Chicago River would have been a small stream draining its own little patch of prairie land and emptying into the Mississippi system. But God, whose sense of humor was working through the glaciers, dumped vast quantities of glacial water, perhaps a quarter of the fresh water in the world, into the middle of those prairie lands. The Lake Michigan–Lake Huron system, geologically one lake and the largest in the world, really doesn't belong in the prairies, but it's here anyhow. As Alderman Hinky Dink Kenna, who hated the lake, remarked, "Why did they build that damn lake next to this city?"

But if it wasn't for the lake, there would be no need for a city. When the railroad system was laid down across the country, the city developed as the natural breaking point between lake traffic and rail traffic. While lake traffic has almost vanished, the railroads are still in place; Chicago continued to be the rail center and later became the air center of the country.

The site of Chicago, the land at the foot of the ridge, was a swamp when the lake was high, indeed an extension of the lake itself toward its old boundaries. In historic times (since the founding of Fort Dearborn) the river normally flowed into the lake. In the last century a heavy rain and the resultant flood swept sewage into the lake and caused a cholera epidemic (in which most of the priests and nuns in Chicago died). The Sanitary and Ship Canal (now called the Water Reclamation District Canal) and the locks at the mouth of the river permanently reversed the flow so that the river now empties into the Mississippi system.

The city of Chicago is permitted by treaty and court decision to divert only a specified amount of water from the lake through the locks at the mouth of the river—even when the lake is at a record high. Hence the city is not able to flush sewage out of the river, so the first Mayor Daley's dream of Loop workers fishing during their lunch hour has not been realized. However, as CBS anchorperson Bill Kurtis pointed out to me (as he prepared for a special on the river), there has been an enormous change in recent years. There is no more legal dumping. New buildings must have riverfront walkways. Brown trout swim in it as casually as they do in Lake Michigan; indeed the river seems to be as pure as Lake Michigan. Plans exist for a walking path all the way to the link between the river and the Water Reclamation District Canal.

The lake you can't miss. The weather reports in the summer tell us that it is cooler near the lake and in the winter that it is warmer near the lake. We flock to its beaches every summer. It is, despite the Hink, part of the ordinary environment of our lives. We take it for granted, miss it when we are away, and wonder why other cities don't have a lake like ours. The most beautiful perspectives in the city are on the lakefront.

Both the Sergeant and I knew that the abandoned Coast Guard station at the breakwater entrance to Chicago harbor had to have a ghost.

"I wouldn't want to go on that boat after dark," the Sergeant said, laughing easily. "But no one has heard anything."

"Indeed."

The three-story, clapboard Victorian station, with a lighthouse cupola, also abandoned, looked like a setting for a thirties Coast Guard movie, set in the Florida Keys, in which the commander and the lieutenant commander were in love with the same woman (maybe the widow of the former commander, who died in the last hurricane). Pressed against the hazy blue late-afternoon sky and the whitecaps pounding against the breakwater, it belonged in San Juan not in Chicago.

—from Happy Are Those Who Thirst for Justice

To the river we pay less attention. Indeed, we are surprised that it shows up so often in films made in Chicago. In the past it was an important part of the industrial and commercial life of the city. In 1900 Chicago was the fourth-busiest port in the world—after New York, London, and Hamburg—and there was a perpetual traffic jam of ships on the river. The ships are gone now; even most of the oar boats that berthed in harbors on the South Side or in Indiana are inactive. An occasional foreign ship is seen at Navy Pier, and some ocean-going vessels tie up in Calumet Harbor. The river has become a highway for occasional barge traffic and for pleasure boats at the beginning and end of the season.

The battered SS *Clipper*, banned from Navy Pier by an irritable city administration, now rests temporarily at the foot of Randolph Street; the future of this last of the lake liners is uncertain at best. We notice the river only when the bridges are raised and traffic on the cross streets is temporarily delayed.

Yet the river is the reason why Chicago came to be, and the early history of the city took place along its banks. More than a few ghosts of the past may still linger there. Brendan Ryan, a man with special psychic propensities, is only too well aware of them.

I don't ask you to believe that such events happen. I will be content for the purposes of this story if you accept as a given that I experience them as happening. Or think I do.

I normally turn left on Wacker and walk to Dearborn. Michigan Avenue is more aesthetically pleasing because of the lake and the park on the left.

However, on that warm April morning, in another century and on the other side of the mountain, I had no time for foolish fantasies.

As best I can remember my state of mind at the time, enough to testify to it in a court of law but hardly enough to convince a psychiatrist, I was not reflecting at all on the southwest corner as the site of Fort Dearborn, the massacre of whose garrison is marked by the first of the four stars in the Chicago flag.

As soon as I crossed the line of the fort's wall, marked by metal studs in the sidewalk, I walked into another century. I saw the garrison leave the fort and begin its fateful trek through the dunes toward the Vincennes Trail (on which I had walked many times as a boy). They would never reach the trail, and only a handful would escape from the ambush that waited at what we now unromantically call 18th Street.

As usual the half-breed scout "Captain" Billy Wells led the way, his face painted black in anticipation of the death that he knew waited for him.

How can I describe for someone who has not had such an experience (technically known as retrocognition) what it is like? The settlers and troops are not ethereal and ectoplasmic creatures. They are as real to me as are the summer-suited pedestrians purposefully rushing along Michigan Avenue with their important and expensive briefcases. I see their worried faces, hear the crying children, sense their fear. Yet the traffic on modern Michigan Avenue does not completely vanish; it fades into the background perhaps, yet it remains. For a few moments I feel that I have a choice between the two worlds, that if I warn them, the garrison and the settlers will not die.

I try to warn them. I choose with futile heroism to abandon 1984 for 1814. It doesn't work. The first Chicagoans fade away slowly, leaving me embarrassed and awkward, wondering if anyone else has seen them and then whether I have made a fool of myself.

—from Rite of Spring

40

The people in my stories are, I think, more aware of the river than most Chicagoans. Red Kane returns to it often, wondering if the transcendental designated hitter who lurks on the river will strike again—and seeking an explanation of the disappearance of his friend Paul O'Meara on the Wabash Avenue (now the Irv Kupcinet) Bridge. In Marina City Red and Eileen Ryan conceived their first child on the day John Kennedy was killed. Red's enemies try to kill him on the lower level of Michigan Avenue near the river. Red himself argues that the lower level and the river are branches of the River Styx and that Charon plies its waters at night. Neil Connor prowls along the river as do Hugh Donlon and Danny Farrell, all of them trying to find meaning for life in its murky waters. The women are less likely to pay attention to the river, though Megan Keefe Lane fishes Neil out of the freezing water a moment before he would drown.

Maybe I prowl the river in imitation of my characters because, like Brendan Ryan, I too am obsessed by the history of the city and the ghosts, benign and malign, that lurk along its bank. Maybe for me the river is the male and the lake the female—even if the flow in the opposite direction kind of ruins the metaphor.

You don't know Chicago, I contend, unless you pay attention to the river.

IV
The Loop

Downtown Chicago is defined by the Loop, even if "downtown" spills beyond the boundaries of Wells (an Indian scout at Fort Dearborn), Van Buren (a president), Wabash (a river), and Lake streets. Most of us think that the name comes from the elevated tracks that run above these streets, though there is some historical reason to believe that even before the elevated tracks were constructed the name was used because of a loop of horse-drawn omnibuses that circled the downtown district.

The L is important to many of my characters, as it was to me when I was growing up.

We had three cars at the house—Dad's old Lasalle, a twin of Ned Ryan's; Mom's new white Olds convertible (in which with her perfectly groomed silver hair and well-maintained figure she attracted considerable attention which flustered and pleased her); and my Roxinante. Still, in those days we routinely used public transportation. The L was a quick and convenient way to ride down town or to Loyola and Quigley. Who needed a car? On an elaborate date with Kate, I'd clean up Roxinante and pick her up in a car; but neither she nor any other girl would complain about an L or streetcar ride to a movie or a nightclub.

—from War in Heaven, *to be published in 1990*

The restored Quincy and Wells L station, the way a station looked when the elevated railway was first constructed.

Inside the Loop one can find some of the most fascinating streets in the world—for example, *Auf Der State Street, dieser fantastischen strasse* as the German translation of *Patience of the Saint* calls it.

If State Street is the "great street," Dearborn is the outdoor museum of the Chicago school of architecture and outdoor sculpture, from South Commons and Printer's Row to Marina City (where John Patrick Kane was conceived out of wedlock the day John Kennedy died and right after Pat Moynihan lamented his lost friend on television) and beyond to Lincoln Park. The central symbol of Dearborn Street is the Picasso in the Richard J. Daley Civic Center Plaza—on which the present mayor looks each day. At Christmas the sculpture is accompanied by a marvelous snowman.

Danny Farrell has his reservations about the Picasso, reservations that I do not share.

It was a mid-February false spring day. Temperatures had soared to the fifties. The ice and snow were melting. Secretaries were eating their lunches on the benches in the Dearborn Street plazas. A few muscial groups had turned up to provide lunch-hour entertainment and prove that summer could not be all that far away.

He strolled with Roger along Dearborn, commenting about the transformation of the street since he had seen it last. He chuckled at the Miró and laughed outright at the Picasso across the street in the Daley Civic Center, which in the Byrne administration, Roger explained, was usually called the Chicago Civic Center.

"Himself was taken in on that one," Danny observed. "He fell for Picasso's joke. But then I suppose if you have to fall for somebody's joke, it might as well be Picasso's."

—*from* Lord of the Dance

58

Technically east of the Loop, but part of it according to most of our own internal maps, is Michigan Avenue, once the lakefront beach. Farther north it becomes the "Magnificent Mile." South of the river it boasts Grank Park (which includes the Petrillo Bandshell and loosely the Goodman Theatre), the Art Institute, Orchestra Hall, the Fine Arts Building, Columbia College, Roosevelt University, Spertus College, the Museum of Judaica, and wondrous (and mysterious) underground garages about which some day I must write a science fiction story. Within sight from the east side of Michigan Avenue, in Grant Park, are the Aquarium, the Planetarium, and the Field Museum of Natural History.

The Cliff Dwellers Club on top of Orchestra Hall is a frequent eating place for my characters, and the concerts in the hall are events to which one might take an important date.

The Cliff Dwellers, scarcely an exclusive and elite club, seemed a magical place to Diana, gentle, a little run-down, civilized, and charming. Orchestra Hall was not run-down; its mixture of red and ivory colors suggested Hapsburg elegance (as she imagined Hapsburg elegance, since the closest she'd been to Vienna was Detroit). Moreover, Sir Georg Solti with his precision direction and his courtly bows also seemed to hint at the Austro-Hungarian Empire.

Diana had the good sense not to admit that she had never been to Orchestra Hall before and to restrain any remark about how much tickets for a box cost.

She did think to herself that his box, empty save for the two of them, would feed a family in Cokewood Springs for a month.

—*from* Love Song

Blackie Ryan is aware of the symbols in the city's outdoor sculpture. After Nick Curran and Catherine Collins triumph over their enemies, he sees the Calder stabile as grinning.

Nicholas and Catherine, Nick and Cathy, would live happily ever after. That is to say, they would have only three or four serious fights each week. Cathy would continue to test him to see if he would take a stand and he would continue to flunk that test most of the time. At least one day a week they would not speak to each other—my homily was beginning to take shape. And on five days their life would be ordinary and routine.

But on the remaining day . . . ah, perhaps on that day they would know the love which is reputed to reflect the Love that launched the universe in a vast BANG.

Maybe even a day and a half some weeks.

Not much, perhaps. Only a little bit—a little bit of light in the gloom, a little bit of life in the entropy, a little bit of love in the indifference.

Maybe that is enough. Maybe, even, it is everything.

That gave me an idea for a Christmas homily, part of which I could also use at the wedding mass.

And as I walked down Dearborn Street in the brightness of a cold crisp December morning, past the grinning Calder flamenco, I heard St. Bernard's Christmas hymn, which said that the little bit of light, the tiny tad of sweetness which is enough, is also everything.

Mane nobiscum Domine
Et nos illustra lumine
Pulsa mentis caligne
Mundum reple dulcedine
Jesu flos matris virginis
Amor nostrae dulcedinis
Tibi laus, honor nominis
Regnum beatitudinis.

—from Virgin and Martyr

Blackie also notes that most of the outdoor sculpture is womanly—the Picasso, the Miró across the street, the Calder, and the Moore in front of the Art Institute. The Dubuffet in front of the ugly State of Illinois building, however, is designed for children of all ages to play in—so Blackie loves to walk under it.

LaSalle Street is the financial center of the city, and the queen of LaSalle, triumphant and majestic at its south end, is the Board of Trade, where Hugh Donlon turns up after he gives up on the priesthood—just down the street from St. Peter's Church, where he went to confession as a priest.

The Chicago Board of Trade was one of the last of the pure marketplaces in the world. Despite the mild regulation provided by the Commodities Exchange Authority of the Department of Agriculture, the "haggling" between buyers and sellers was more sustained and more frantic than it would have been in an Oriental bazaar where "real" objects were sold. In the trading pits no physical objects changed hands. The traders bought and sold "futures"—consignments of commodities that the traders never saw and never owned.

They spoke their own language, shouting fractions at one another and waving their hands to indicate whether they were selling or buying contracts, aided by hand signals that indicated the fraction of the trading price they were bidding or offering. Dressed in light, colored blazers, they swarmed around their "pit," one of the three-step platforms constructed on the trading floor. They scrawled sales contracts on small sheets of paper, which they dropped on the floor to be snatched by messengers and coordinated later in the day by the "Clearing Corporation," the self-policing and account-balancing organization that prevented the chaos of the trading floor from degenerating into anarchy.

—*from* Ascent into Hell

South of the Loop, on the shores of the lake, is Soldier Field, where the Bears play. All my characters (women as well as men) are Bear fans, with the exception of such silently loyal Chicago Cardinal fans as Ned Ryan and Chuck O'Malley—innocents who stand by the Cardinals even after they transferred themselves first to St. Louis and then to Phoenix.

When the Bears played in the Superbowl, the Ryans wrote their own version of "The Superbowl Shuffle."

> *"I'm Father Blackie and I say the mass.*
> *I preach and sing, without much class.*
> *The Cardinal will tell you I'm A-OK*
> *So long as I do whatever he say.*
> *I've cheered the Bears all my life;*
> *If they don't win for me, they're not nice.*
> *I promise God that She'll get no trouble*
> *'Long as the Bears take the Super Bowl Shuffle!"*

—*from* All About Women

V
Blackie's Neighborhood

Blackie Ryan presides over the city from the river to Lincoln Park, Holy Name Cathedral parish. It's his turf.

I followed the Indian paths through my parish, down Superior Street to the Olson Pavilion, then over Fairbanks Court, Chicago Avenue, and Seneca Court to Delaware Street, the John Hancock on the left, the Westin on the right, back up to the corner of Delaware and Michigan. Straight ahead, half a block down, behind the Fourth Presbyterian Church was the Whitehall, and right behind it, on Chestnut, across from Quigley Seminary, the Tremont. Around on my left, across Chestnut Street, was the Carlton. On my right, down Michigan Avenue, on the other side of the Playboy (ugh, I said that word) building, was the good, gray Drake. And around the corner, a few steps down east Lake Shore Drive, the chic Mayfair. Everyone literally within a stone's throw of the Westin. A five-minute walk or, at the most, a two- or three-minute run. Sister Winnie up Lake Shore Drive in Rogers Park in her commune, but at 9:30 at night, no more than a fifteen-minute drive down Lake Shore and onto Michigan, stopping right in front of the Westin. Fran Leonard in his office at the First Illinois building on La Salle Street, ten minutes by cab from Michigan and Delaware. Any and all of these people could have been out on the fog-crowded streets that trail away like lesser canyons from the Magnificent Mile.

—from Happy Are the Clean of Heart

Neil Connor takes Megan Lane to the Ice Cream Studio, which is also one of Blackie's favorite hangouts.

They stopped in front of the Ice Cream Studio.
"I think they built this place in the Cathedral parish," Neal held the door for her, "so that our friend the Monsignor could have the best malts in the city a few steps from his rectory."
"Maybe he owns it . . . why do they call it a studio?"
"Look at the paintings."
She glanced around, "Matisse, Picasso, Seurat prints, what's so . . . oh, my heavens, they're all eating ice cream!"
"A delicious joke, wouldn't you say?"
"Shame on you," she thumped his arm lightly.
"Delicious joke, delicious ice cream, delicious woman."
"You're like totally gross," she mimicked Teri. "May I have an extra large one, please. Lent will start after Christmas."
"I hope not."

—*from* Valentine's Night

The cardinal and Blackie walked down Michigan Avenue toward Superior Street, a venture that on a warm day in mid-September compared favorably with a walk along the French Riviera. Sean Cronin, however, was distracted by problems.

They paused at the window of the Wally Findlay Galleries, across from that old wedding cake phony, the Water Tower. They were showing Philip Auge—sensuous alabaster women, cool, remote, and draped in gorgeous gowns, appropriately for a former fashion designer.

—from Angels of September

I donned my World War II aviator's jacket and a fake navy commander's cap, which had "BOSS" emblazoned on it in gold letters, and, with George Quinn's manuscript under my arm, sallied forth from the rectory down Wabash and turned on Chicago Avenue toward the lake. October is the finest month in the year for our city, which, together with Florence and Hong Kong and San Francisco, is one of the four most beautiful cities in the world. In rapid succession, as though racing to finish their performance before the cold of winter comes, there follow foggy, humid days with no wind; brisk, clear, cloudless days with the northeast wind stirring up nervous whitecaps on the lake and driving crystalline air across the city; and then the most magical interlude of all, Indian summer, when a golden haze settles on the city and paints everything elegiac. On those days the poets in Chicago (of which I am not one) do half their work of the year and the philosophers in Chicago (of which I am one) do half their thinking of the year. That morning, however, was of the second rather than the third variety: a brisk, clean, deep-blue autumn morning of the sort on which even professional cynics have a hard time not being happy. Should Chicago weather be like that every day of the year, no one in the world would live anyplace else.

I parked myself in one of my favorite places for philosophical reflection, a little park across from the Water Tower, surrounded by the giant canyon walls of the John Hancock Center, Water Tower Place, the partially finished Olympia Center ("Needless Mark-up Building" my nieces call it, taunting Neiman-Marcus's prices) and—substantially less tall—Loyola University. It's an arena of pure privacy, despite the rushing traffic, human and nonhuman, surging back and forth on Michigan Avenue. The pedestrians who see a funny little man hunched over a manuscript on a park bench have two choices: if they don't know who he is, they leave him alone because he looks, as the teenagers say, "like, kinda weird, right?" And if they do know him, they dismiss him with a laugh, "Oh, Monsignor Blackie is thinking again!"

I permit them that illusion.

—from Happy Are the Clean of Heart

The first six floors of the building are a monumental shopping plaza, space for urban teenagers to "mall crawl"—an apparently biologically programmed behavior of the species—and, with Lord & Taylor, Marshall Field, Kroch's and Brentano's, and F.A.O. Schwarz scattered conveniently about, an ideal locale for a cathedral cleric to do his last (and first) Christmas shopping on Christmas Eve.

I rode to the top floor of the shopping plaza and entered an Accent Chicago store, where I purchased a Chicago Cubs jacket that I thought might make an appropriate addition to the color of the "Monsignor Blackie" wardrobe. It would hang next to the Quigley Seminary jacket I had worn for twenty years and which, my female siblings claim, has never once been cleaned.

"Aren't you going to buy a Chicago Bears jacket, Monsignor Blackie?" asked the young person behind the counter, a red-haired, green-eyed little person whom I did not recognize.

"If they beat Tampa Bay next Sunday, they will certainly win their division," I temporized with her, "and then I might add one of their jackets to my collection, too."

"What if the Bulls and the Sting and the Blackhawks and Northwestern and even the University of Chicago win championships?"

"I will get down on my knees and pray because I will know that the Day is at hand!"

The redhead, and all the other young persons in the Accent Chicago shop, squealed merrily. As Mrs. Chesterton said of G.K., "If you cannot make him attractive, then at least make him colorful."

Or, in more modern parlance, there are various dimensions of "cute."

—from Happy Are the Clean of Heart

Others besides the little monsignor walk the streets of the neighborhood. Jim O'Neill contemplates the cardinal's mansion—in which Sean Cronin, my cardinal, does not live (he stays in the cathedral rectory, where he can give his famous instruction "Blackwood, see to it."), although the cardinal in God's world does live there.

Victorian fog oozed in off Lake Michigan and turned Lincoln Park into gloomy moorland. Well, it seemed Victorian or even Holmesian as it slipped past the archbishop's multi-chimneyed house—he counted twenty-six of them. Someday he would have to write a Holmesian story; the gloom fit his mood. What better place than a moor to treasure guilt feelings? He rose from the park bench and walked along North Avenue toward Clark Street, glancing at his watch again. Why had he come so early? Another half-hour to go.

According to the young priest—Uncle Mike, Micky, whatever—the archbishop had tried to sell the house as part of his continual financial maneuvers only to discover that the land was owned by the Mercy Sisters, bought for a previous archbishop by his sister who was a mother general. The modern Mercys didn't object to building a high-rise condo on the land, only they wouldn't give the money to His Prominence . . . stalemate. Somehow an angular condo wouldn't look nearly so appropriate across from the park as the old Victorian monstrosity.

—*from* Death in April

Anne O'Brien and Mike Casey, long-separated lovers, wander through the neighborhood after they have renewed their love.

They ate at an ice-cream bar in the park and then returned to her apartment via North State Parkway and Astor Street, enjoying the courtly charm of the Gold Coast's most expensive homes, whose trees were tentatively turning red under the sweet and soft Indian summer sky. It was the sort of setting in which, if it were not for the large imported cars parked bumper to bumper, one might expect to encounter Henry James or some of his characters. Then they walked down Michigan Avenue, gawking at the tall buildings gleaming silver in the sunlight.

—*from* Angels of September

Larry Burke, Sue, and Laurel—some of the many people who leave through the same doorway—leave the cathedral rectory and walk out into the autumn air to begin their new life with Blackie's uneasy benediction.

The three of them, Sue in the middle, guarded by her two protectors as she approached her fabled sophomore slump twenty-four years late, walked happily north on Wabash, toward Chicago Avenue, in the balmy warmth of their love and the warmth of the September sun. For the moment no dark and evil bird lurked behind them.

In the memorable words of O'Connor The Cat, "Summer is over but life goes on."

—*from* Happy Are the Meek

I imagine this to be Red Kane's family home.

VI
Red Kane's Neighborhood

North of Blackie's neighborhood—from Lincoln Park to Wrigley Field—and as far west as Ashland Avenue (and even beyond) is the domain of the professional and managerial class that has elected to stay in the city, including Redmond Peter Kane and his family. The family of his wife, Eileen, has elected to stay in Beverly, and his grammar school friends have left behind North Austin for Oak Park and River Forest. Red and Eileen, however, have chosen the city, like many of their generation and many, many more of the next generation. Once the bailiwick of the lakefront limousine liberals (and reformers!), the area west and north of Lincoln Park has changed as dramatically as any in the city. Halsted Street has become the main street of yuppiedom (where there live not only yuppies but also yicups—young Irish Catholic urban professionals). The old ethnic communities, threatened with urban renewal, find themselves instead the target for gentrification. Much of the hope for the future of the city rests on how successful this westward-moving mix of social classes will be.

St. Josephat's on Southport, near the western border of yuppiedom.

Long before Red and Eileen Kane moved into Lincoln Park, Jerry Keenan in 1946 followed his recently rediscovered love, Maggie Ward.

I waited in the lobby of the Drake till the restaurant closed, collected my wermacht coat, which over my pinstripe suit made me a different person, and hung around near the door that the help at the Drake used to exit. I pulled my stocking cap down over my ears, partly for disguise but mostly to keep warm. I waited for several millennia, though my watch said it was only a half hour. Several other young women left the hotel, but I was restrained this time—no staring into astonished faces. I would know Maggie's walk.

And I did. She walked briskly, as the cold demanded, but also as if she were carrying a heavy burden in addition to the small purse and paper shopping bag.

She crossed Michigan on Walton, walked by the 900 Michigan apartment building and, scarf pulled tightly around her head and thin, cloth coat buttoned to the top, hurried through the cold and lonely darkness across Rush and State and Dearborn, around the top of Bughouse (actually Union) Square in the shadow of the Newberry Library, to the Clark Street car stop.

I walked twenty or thirty yards behind her, trying to silence the hobnail-like thump of my combat boots on the snow. But Maggie didn't seem to be listening, either because she was too tired or because she had made her peace with the dangers and refused to worry.

It was a long wait for one of the new, streamlined Clark Street cars, which had already been named, not inappropriately, Green Hornets. I huddled in the door of the library, noted that we were again under the light of a full moon, and tried to keep my fingers from falling off.

Maggie reached in her shopping bag, produced a book, and under the streetlight on Clark Street on December 23, no, it was already Christmas Eve 1946, calmly read while waiting for a Green Hornet.

When the car finally came, she closed the book around her finger, paid the conductor the required seven cents, walked halfway up the almost empty car, and sank wearily into a seat.

I followed her, again noisily and clumsily, sat a couple of seats behind her, and strained my perfectly good aviator's eyes to see what she was reading.

Carlo Levi. Christ Stopped at Eboli.

Unquestionably an intellectual. Now if she only proved to be a Democrat.

We got off at North Avenue, crossed the street, and boarded the ancient red streetcar, which would branch off from Clark and go up Lincoln. It was much colder inside the car than in the toasty-warm Green Hornet.

Maggie was too absorbed in her book to notice the highly suspicious young man who was following her.

There were only two other people in the car—aged cleaning women probably returning from their jobs in Loop office buildings. I felt sad for them too. But unlike my Maggie, they would celebrate Christmas with their families, not merely painful memories.

The car moved rapidly through the winter night. We crossed Halsted, then Fullerton, and chugged by the grounds of McCormick Theological Seminary. Maggie returned Carlo Levi to her shopping bag, walked a little less briskly to the front of the car, and spoke to the driver. He stopped at the next corner, Sheffield, just north of Wrightwood. I moved to the center door. Maggie got off and turned automatically up Sheffield. I followed behind her as an Evanston L train roared by on tracks behind the two-flats and apartment buildings on our right.

Now the neighborhood is at the heart of Near Northwest Side yuppiedom. Then it was a German and Swedish ethnic community, not quite yet picturesque, fading off into the edges of poverty but still stable and safe, though perhaps not perfectly safe for an eighteen-year-old girl in the early hours of the morning. The northern-most finger of the Chicago fire had reached into the neighborhood, eliminating all but a few of the wooden buildings. The sidewalks were raised later as part of the city's struggle out of the swamp of mud on which it was built, but first floors below ground level and second floor entrances remained as relics of the swampy days at the turn of the century. Even many of the postfire, stone three-flats with pointed roofs, evidence of the German influence, had second-story entrances.

Then it was an ugly neighborhood; now we think it has character.

Halfway up the block, Maggie turned into a wooden, prefire three-flat. She climbed up the stairs, opened the second floor entrance, and went in. That meant she lived on either the second or the third floor. First-floor residents would walk down to the entrance on the old ground level below the sidewalk.

My brain roaring with a noise louder than a thousand L trains, I walked by the house, turned short of the corner of Shubert Avenue by a church that I noted was St. George's Greek Orthodox, returned quickly to her three-flat, and climbed the slippery wooden steps. There were four apartments on the third floor, small, small flats. Next to one of the doorbells, neatly printed, was the name for which I had been searching since August—"M. M. Ward."

I must have hesitated five minutes, shuddering with the cold, before I worked up enough nerve to push the buzzer.

"Yes?" She replied promptly, still wide awake.

"Andrea King?"

Total silence.

"Or should I say Margaret Koenig?"

More silence.

"Would Maggie Ward do?"

"Go away."

"I will not, even if I freeze to death."

"I don't want to talk to you."

"You don't have to talk to me. I must return some money to you."

"Money?"

"I don't take loan-shark rates. You owe me only a dollar and a half interest. I figure I'm entitled to a fifty-cent service charge. So I have eight dollars to return to you. I don't want it on my conscience when I receive Communion at midnight mass tomorrow . . . no, tonight."

The buzzer rang.

Maggie Ward lived in the attic of a house like this.

Inside the apartment Jerry observes the poverty that existed in the neighborhood at that time.

Underneath the robe she was wearing heavy pink pajamas to keep warm in the chilly if bravely cheerful cave in which she lived. It was a single room with a small kitchen alcove and a tiny bathroom without a shower or a tub. An old-fashioned coal heater, converted to gas, occupied one corner of the room, a sealed gaslight fixture on the wall. A bed, a table, a dilapidated mohair chair, and a paperboard wardrobe constituted the furniture underneath a ceiling bulb in another old gaslight fixture. Piles of books lined the walls, and a stack of notebooks rested against the chair.

My kids would not believe that such an apartment could exist in Chicago outside the slums, but in the middle 1940s there were tens of thousands of such places without central heating or shower or tub. They were modified cold-water apartments, with a toilet and a washbasin installed in a crudely partitioned little compartment, but the bathtub was in the next apartment or one of the others on the floor. You had to ask permission to use it and perhaps pay for the hot water. Maggie was more fortunate than most who lived in such places because there was surely a shower for waitresses somewhere in the bowels of the Drake. A mile or two farther south, in the Polish neighborhood between Division Street and North Avenue, there were still outdoor privies and buildings without bath facilities whose residents had to use the public bathhouses that the city provided (one of which was made famous in a Saul Bellow novel). Even after the war many Chicagoans thought themselves fortunate to find such a cave in which to live.

It was easy for the social critics like Pete Seeger a few years later to make fun of the "ticky tac" suburban houses, which were springing up on the fringes of most of the cities of the country. But Seeger was a rich kid who went to Harvard. He never lived in a cold-water flat. So he never knew the joy of having for the first time your own bathroom and separate bedrooms for the different members of the family.

Like many other women in such places, or worse places, Maggie had done her best to make it look bright and comfortable. The coverlet on the bed, turned down now, was a bright floral print, the inexpensive throw rug a bright green. A miniature Christmas tree with a single string of lights glowed on the table next to a small crib set. A bright picture of sun and beach was tacked to one wall and a print of a Raphael madonna smiled benignly from the other panel of wall space. Crowded, cold, and uncomfortable, the apartment was nonetheless impeccably neat, a stern warning that its occupant would tolerate neither disorder nor nonsense.

Some women, my wife says, not without contempt, have order in their homes and nothing else.

"I'll turn up the heat." Maggie bent over the stove. "Can't have you freezing to death."

They argue about their love. Jerry is able to move her a little away from her stubborn insistence that it has no future. Then . . .

I was about to applaud her wisdom when the apartment was shaken by what seemed to be a massive Christmas Eve earthquake and a roar that sounded like a hundred Pratt and Whitney's.

"Don't be afraid; it's only the L," she laughed. "Your great Chicago institution. I kind of like it. I think it keeps me company."

I waited for the rolling apocalypse to pass and returned to my argument.

—from War in Heaven, *to be published in 1990*

The L tracks outside Maggie Ward's window.

St. Clement's, Red Kane's parish church.

Forty years later Red Kane rides home on the bus after his experience by the green glass skyscraper. As the bus approaches Webster, he reads from the poet Richard Wilbur—whose lines sum up my vision of the city as sacrament.

> . . . oh maculate, cracked, askew,
> Gay-pocked and potsherd world
> I voyage, where in every tangible tree
> I see afloat among the leaves, all calm and curled,
> The Cheshire smile—which sets me fearfully free.

—*from* Patience of a Saint

Much has changed from the apartment of Maggie Ward to the home of Red Kane, but hunger for love and fear of it are the same. (In *Love Song* Red Kane attends Maggie's sixtieth birthday party, so they obviously came to know one another. I wonder if they talked about the neighborhood. Probably.)

Red tries to run from love as well as Love, or God, but the latter won't let him escape. At Christmas Mass in St. Clement's Church the cosmic designated hitter strikes again.

The choir, disgracefully well trained, shifted from "O Little Town of Bethlehem" to "Silent Night," the church lights dimmed, candles blazed on the altar, their reflections bouncing off the poinsettias like shimmering waves seen from a vast deserted beach at sunset, a floodlight illumined the crib.

All the familiar Midnight Mass gimmickry, *he thought, ignoring the lump in his throat.* Not much of a church but great theater. *"We're going to sing 'Adeste Fideles' as our entrance hymn," said the young priest in the sanctuary. "When Father Fahey and other ministers of the Eucharist come down the aisle, they represent all of us who are the faithful hastening to Bethlehem. The crib is Bethlehem for us at Midnight Mass of course, but we should remember that the altar is Bethlehem every day of the year, the place where the world is renewed."*

—*from* Patience of a Saint

The inside of St. Clement's, where Red has his Christmas experience.

St. Ursula's Church, which, in the story, Chuck O'Malley's father designed and where Chuck and Rosie were married.

VII
Hugh Donlon's Neighborhood

The St. Ursula's parish of my novels is in fact the St. Angela's parish of real life, the neighborhood of Hugh Donlon—and Anne O'Brien, Mike Casey, Ned Ryan before he went off to war (I don't know why he committed the treasonous felony of moving to the South Side when he came home), Chuck O'Malley and his family, and the legendary Monsignor Martin D. ("Mugsy") Branigan.

Before we see Mugsy at work, let's observe some of his parishioners in 1945. A nun at St. Ursula has banned Rosemarie Clancy from the role of May crowning queen, to which she had been elected, and appointed Chuck O'Malley's sister to replace Rosemarie. April O'Malley, Chuck's mother, plans to fight back.

There was a long delay before the door opened—it is an unwritten rule of the Catholic church (as yet unrepealed) that no convent or rectory door can be opened without a maddening wait being imposed on the one who has disturbed ecclesiastical peace by ringing the bell.

Sister Mary Admiral did not answer the door, of course. Mothers Superior did not do that sort of thing. The nun who did answer, new since my day in grammar school, kept her eyes averted as she showed us into the parlor, furnished in the heavy green style of pre–World War I with three popes, looking appallingly feminine, watching us with pious simpers.

The nameless nun scurried back with a platter on which she had arrayed butter cookies, fudge, two small tumblers, and a pitcher of lemonade.

"Don't eat them all, Chucky," Mom warned me as we waited for Mother Superior to descend upon us.

"I won't," I lied.

The convent cookies and fudge—reserved for visitors of special importance—were beyond reproach. I will confess, however, that I was the one responsible for the story that when the lemonade had been sent to a chemist for analysis, he had reported with great regret that our poor horse was dying of incurable kidney disease.

"April, dear, how wonderful to see you!" the War Admiral came in swinging. "You look wonderful. Painting airplanes certainly agrees with you." She hugged Mom. "And Charles . . . my, how you've grown!"

I hadn't. But I did not reply because the last bit of fudge had followed the final cookie into my digestive track.

The War Admiral launched her campaign quickly, hook nose almost bouncing against jutting chin as she spit out her carefully prepared lines. "I'm so sorry about this little misunderstanding. Your precious Margaret Mary should be the one to crown the Blessed Mother. She is such a darling, so good and virtuous and popular. I often worry about her friendship with the Clancy child. I'm afraid that she's a bad influence. I hope you don't regret their friendship someday."

"Oh, Sister, I would be so unhappy if Peg did not graduate from St. Ursula next month, just as Jane and Chuck, uh, Charles here did."

Oh, boy.

"But there's no question of that . . ."

Mom ignored her. "The sisters out at Trinity did tell me that they'll accept her as a freshman with a music scholarship even if she doesn't graduate."

"But . . ."

"And, as sad as it would be to break my husband's heart," Mom seemed close to tears, "I'll have to withdraw Peg from St. Ursula if she is put in this impossible situation."

"She wouldn't come back to school anyway," I added helpfully, licking the last trace of fudge from my lips.

"Shush, darling," Mom murmured.

"My dear," the Admiral's voice was sweet and oily, "we really can't let the Clancy girl crown Our Blessed Lady. Her father is a criminal and her mother . . . well, as I'm sure you know," her voice sunk to a whisper, "she drinks!"

"All the more reason to be charitable to Rosemarie."

"Like Jesus to Mary Magdalene," I added helpfully.

"Shush, darling."

"Monsignor Meany established very firm rules for this honor."

"Monsignor Meany is dead, God be good to him."

"Cold in his grave," I observed.

"His rules will remain in force as long as I am superior."

"Time for a change, I guess," I murmured.

"You give me no choice but to visit Monsignor Branigan."

"Please yourself."

The warm night had turned frigid.

"I shall."

"Don't say anything, dear," Mom said as we walked down Menard Avenue to the front door of the rectory. "Not a word."

"Who, me?"

St. Ursula's Convent, where April and Sister Admirabilis battled.

April and Chuck go to the rectory.

After the routine wait for the bell to be answered, we were admitted to a tiny office littered with baptismal books. Monsignor Branigan, in black clerical suit, appeared almost at once, medium height, thick glasses, red face, and broad smile.

"April Cronin!" he exclaimed, embracing her—unheard of behavior from a priest in those days. "Greetings and salutations! You look more beautiful than ever!"

"April Mae Cronin," I observed.

They knew each other, did they? Sure they did. All South Side Irish knew one another.

I glance at pictures I took of her at that time. Yes, indeed, Monsignor Mugsy was right.

"Great," the Monsignor exclaimed. "Now, April, what's on your mind?"

Mom told him.

"Dear God," he breathed out and reclined in his swivel chair, "how can we do things like this to people? Some day we're going to have to pay a terrible price."

"Mary Magdalene . . ." I began.

"Shush, darling."

"You two are willing to vouch for the poor little tyke?"

"Certainly," Mom nodded vigorously. "She's a lovely child."

"You bet," I perjured myself because I thought my life might depend on it.

"Well, that settles that."

The Monsignor threw up his hands. "See what's happening to the church, April? Well, go home and tell Peggy—I know which one she is, she looks like you did when you crowned the Blessed Mother at St. Gabe's—that her friend will do the honors next week."

A woman's study in River Forest, not unlike the one that Rosemarie Clancy O'Malley designed for herself.

Chuck has his problems at the May crowning.

Just as Rosie raised the circle of blossoms, I saw an absolutely perfect shot frozen in my viewfinder. I pushed the shutter button, the bulb exploded, the ladder swayed, and Rosemarie Helen Clancy fell off it.

On me.

I found myself, dazed and sore, on the sanctuary floor, buried in a swirl of bridal lace and disordered feminine limbs.

"Are you all right?" she demanded. "Did I hurt you?"

"I'm dead, you clumsy goof."

"It's all your fault," Peg snarled, pulling Rosie off me. "You exploded that flash thing deliberately."

I struggled to my feet to be greeted by an explosion of laughter.

What's so funny, I wondered as every hand bell in every nunnish hand in the church clanged in dismay.

Then I felt the flowers on my head. Rosie had crowned not the Blessed Mother, but me.

Even the frightened little train bearers were snickering.

I knew I had better rise to the occasion or I was dead in the neighborhood and at Fenwick High School.

Forever and ever.

Amen.

So I bowed deeply to the giggling Rosie and with a single motion, swept the flowers off my wire-brush hair and into her hand. She bowed back.

She may have winked too, for which God forgive her.

These days Catholic congregations applaud in church on almost any occasion, even for that rare event, the good sermon. In those days applause in the sacred confines was unthinkable.

Nonetheless, led by Monsignor Branigan and Father Raven, the whole church applauded.

Except for the nuns, who were pounding frantically on their hand bells.

Rosie darted up the ladder just in time to put the crown where it belonged. As she turned to descend, the ladder tottered again. I steadied it with my left hand and helped her down with my right.

She blushed and smiled at me.

And owned the whole world.

The O'Malley's were poor in the Great Depression, a fact that bothered Chuck more than his parents.

Our flat was small and cramped. Before 1938 our ice was delivered through a hatch on the back porch. We kids hated the day our secondhand Serval refrigerator appeared because we knew we would miss the iceman, who lugged blocks of ice up the stairs on his back and dumped them through the "ice door." He always had a kind word and a joke for us, poor man, too old for such hard work but knowing no other way to earn his living.

For Mom the fridge was a welcome relief from some of the worries and strains of housework—an ironing board in the kitchen, walks up and down four flights of stairs to the basement to a primitive washer with a hand-operated "wringer" through whose rollers clothes were passed after they were washed, heavy clothes baskets to drag out into the concrete backyard, laundry hung by wooden clothespins on lines that had to be put up after each washing, hot-water heat in noisy radiators fed by a coal furnace that left a fine layer of dark dust on everything in the house.

We were better off than many. We had inside plumbing, and our dark apartment was lit by enough electric lights (some fixed to the now-unused gas jets) that one could read after dark. But Mom had never lifted a finger at housework until the crash.

If the setbacks bothered her, she never let anyone else know about her discouragement. "Refinement," she told us often, "has nothing to do with how much money you have or where you live. It's part of your character."

The sort of apartment building in which the O'Malleys lived.

The kind of bungalow in which the Donlons lived.

The corner drugstore that was a hangout for the young men of the parish.

The Rockne Theater, where Hugh and Chuck and many others went to the movies. It later became an emporium for X-rated films and is now a Baptist church.

Not all the young people in the parish were as innocuous as Chuck O'Malley. Consider the escapades of Terry Dunn.

It was this unecumenical activity that finally brought the career of the Gray Ghost to an end. There was some very important function at the local Missouri Synod Lutheran congregation. Terry and Julie got a chorus of thirty papists to stand across the street singing hymns to the Blessed Mother all evening long. The police were called, but in 1942, what Irish cop was going to put kids in jail for praising the Blessed Mother?

The Lutheran pastor went to see the Monsignor in solemn high procession, an unheard-of event, and the Monsignor, who knew nothing of the exploits of the Gray Ghost, gave the young curate strict instructions to "stop that blasphemy." The young curate knew all about the band of the Gray Ghost but had minded his own business. Now he laid down the law.

—*from* All About Women

The Lutheran church across the street from the Donlon house. The church was the target of the Gray Ghost and his companions.

For those of us who moved into the bungalow belt from apartment buildings during the later years of the Depression, the bungalows seemed ideal homes. But in the years after the war, many of the parishioners who now had more money and larger families moved into the suburbs, particularly those to the west of us—Oak Park and River Forest. The O'Malley's, Maria Manfredi McLain, and lots of others became suburbanites. St. Luke's in River Forest became a kind of reincarnation of St. Angela's.

The big bungalow at the corner of Lemoyne and Mason was beginning to show its age, along with the rest of the St. Ursula's neighborhood. Many of the parishioners had migrated to River Forest as black families moved into the south end of the parish. The decline of the neighborhood and the deterioration of his family home depressed Hugh. But even with the burden of Liz on his mind, he could hardly wait to be inside.

—from Ascent into Hell

A home like the one where Chuck and Rosie lived after they were married.

It was at the entrance of one of those River Forest homes that Hugh Donlon finally understood his own life.

Her house loomed behind her—trimly painted gables, a soft light in the parlor window, the kindly glow of dusk reflected in the other windows. A house he had never entered. Yet he knew it well enough—neat, clean, warm, uncoventional furniture, and flamboyant decorations. A pleasant house, inviting, reassuring, comforting. And once you went into its light you never left. Mason Avenue, Lake Geneva, Bethlehem.

—*from* Ascent into Hell

VIII
Noele Farrell's Neighborhood

Tucked in a far corner of the southwest side, Beverly is on top of the Chicago Ridge, which is the Continental Divide and the highest point in Cook County. At the foot of the ridge is Longwood Drive (sometimes called Glenwood Drive in my stories), which is the old Vincennes Trail out of Chicago. St. Praxides (Christ the King in God's world) is the neighborhood of most of the people in my stories—the Farrells, the Ryans, Neil Connor, Megan Keefe, Lisa Malone, and Catherine Collins Curran.

Listen to Neil Connor describe it.

In his dreams about the neighborhood, Neal had pictured it as deteriorating into a resegregated slum, a fate he told himself that it richly deserved, just as a hated woman deserved to grow old and ugly. He had been surprised when the lovely Lisa, singer, actress, and now producer, had told him that it was still flourishing as an integrated community. "More whites than blacks moving in," she had smiled, "homes going for three hundred to four hundred thousand dollars."

Neal had been skeptical, but his quick drive from 95th Street to the Woods and back convinced him. The Dutch Colonial, Tudor, and old Victorian homes (some of them a hundred years old now) seemed as well-maintained as ever. The dowager homes on the ridge above Longwood Drive still looked down superciliously on the the small park next to the Rock Island Station, conscious no doubt that they stood on the highest point in Cook County and that the Drive was the historic Vincennes Trail.

The Ravine, a gully cut through sand dunes thousands of years ago was still picturesque, virtually the only wooded hills in Chicago; its homes clung to the sides of the ancient dunes like they were in a Swiss village. And St. Praxides, one of the first of the modern churches built after the war, still kept a watchful eye on the community with its yellow brick elegance untarnished.

A magic neighborhood, the young priest had said when Neal was in high school.
"Spoiled rich neighborhood," Neal had sneered.
"You sound like a walking cliche," the priest had snapped back.
Not nearly so devious and indirect a cleric as Blackie Ryan . . .

—from Valentine's Night

For Noele Farrell the center of the parish is the basketball and volleyball courts.

The trees on the curving streets of the Neighborhood, which Noele thought was the most totally cool place in the world, were turning red, reminding her of the vestments the priests wore at Mass on Pentecost. And the big oaks around the Courts were pure gold, making the sun-drenched asphalt look like a grove. Noele, who loved Latin and was upset that the nuns didn't teach Greek anymore, insisted that the Courts were sacred. They were the center of the parish. When the kids said, "Let's go over to St. Prax's," they meant not the church but the Courts.

Sacred grove or not, the Courts were devoid not only of cute boys but all boys. Only Father Ace was there, still trying to dunk, and at his age. . . .

—*from* Lord of the Dance

I danced in the morning
When the world was begun,
I danced in the moon
And the stars and the sun.
I came down from heaven
And I danced on the earth,
At Bethlehem
I had My birth.
Dance, then,
Wherever you may be,
I am the Lord
Of the Dance, said He.
I'll lead you all
Wherever you may be,
I'll lead you all
In the Dance, said He.

I danced for the scribes
And the Pharisees,
But they would not dance,
They wouldn't follow Me.
I danced for the fisherman,
For James and John,
They came with Me
And the dance went on.

I danced on a Friday
When the sky turned black,
It's hard to dance
With the devil on your back.
They buried My body
And they thought I'd gone,
But I am the dance
And I still go on.

They cut Me down
And I leap up high,
I am the life
That'll never, never die.
I live in you
If you live in Me,
I am the Lord
Of the Dance, said He.

Dance, then,
Wherever you may be,
I am the Lord
Of the Dance, said He.
I'll lead you all
Wherever you may be,
I'll lead you all
In the Dance, said He.

—song "Lord of the Dance" by Sidney Carter,
used in Lord of the Dance

160

161

And having been violated by those who hurt her, Noele returns to the courts to find meaning.

Then Noele saw a broad beam of sunlight move lazily down Jefferson Avenue, like a sophomore girl slouching home from the Ninety-fifth Street bus on a warm, Indian summer afternoon, daydreaming about a senior boy to whom she had never spoken a word in her life. Dark clouds moved ahead of the sun as though running from it, and Jefferson Avenue was bright all the way to Ninety-fifth Street.

—from Lord of the Dance

She insists that the music in church be done properly—that is to say, her way.

You don't have a proper teenage folk Mass when the D. O. M. and two other retards sing a Mozart trio during Communion. Noele had nothing personal against Mozart, poor man; however, a Mozart trio during Communion wiped out the congregation's enthusiasm for singing, which the folk group had diligently stirred up earlier in the Mass. It was hard enough to get Catholics to sing in church as it was without pouring water on a weak fire with old Wolfgang Amadeus.

Moreover, the final hymn was "Lord of the Dance," Noele's favorite. She couldn't bear to have it sung listlessly.

Father Ace, who said the 9:15 Mass every Sunday, gave the final blessing. As he was urging the congregation to go forth in the peace of Christ, Noele slipped up to the microphone on the left-hand side of the sanctuary, beating the slow-moving Director of Music by three feet.

"Our final hymn is 'Lord of the Dance.'" Michele Carmody and the other kids began to hum the familiar melody, which was the same as that of "Simple Gifts." Noele plunged on, like a dolphin that has surfaced and then dives back into the water. "Our lives are a dance, and our friends and families are our dancing partners, and God is the head of the dance. He calls the tunes, and directs the music, and invites us all to dance. Sometimes He even interrupts our normal dances so that He can dance just with us. Let's all sing it like we were dancing so that God will know that we are ready to dance with Him whenever He wants."

Congressman and Mrs. Burns and all the little Burns kids in the second row of the church looked startled. Jaimie rolled his Robert Redford eyes. Father Ace laughed, and behind her the Director of Music coughed as if he were ready to die. Noele didn't budge an inch. Standing at the microphone, strumming vigorously on her guitar, she led the thousand assembled Christians in a rendition of "Lord of the Dance" that made the walls of the long, cool, modern church shake with excitement.

—from Lord of the Dance

165

Lisa Malone and George Quinn (George the Bean Counter) meet one another at the 91st Street station and are joined by Caitlin Murphy.

It might have been better, all things considered, if she had descended on the neighborhood with a limo, a chauffeur, a maid, a mink coat, two French poodles, a press agent, and several trunks full of clothes. Even my mother would have been impressed, although offended. Lisa elected to return as the same old Lisa, riding the Rock Island (still called that even if it is owned by the RTA) in brown slacks, sweater, scarf, and beige cloth coat, wearing no makeup and carrying her own garment bag, a pretty young woman returning for Christmas, perhaps from graduate school. We met at the end of the car as we prepared to exit at the 91st Street station. I had seen her as soon as she boarded the car, of course, and knew that I wouldn't open my book of Paul Claudel's plays on that ride.

Blackie would have said of me that I was twenty years ahead of my time: I was thinking the thoughts of the 1950s about the books of the 1930s. . . .

—*from* Happy Are the Clean of Heart

Caitlin's father, Joseph Murphy, M.D. (from Boston), tells us about the beginning of his romance with her mother, Mary Kathleen Ryan, M.D., at Little Company of Mary Hospital. The latter, a med school student, had made the former's life miserable during her six weeks under his supervision at LCM.

She also scared the hell out of me.

"Miss Ryan?"

"Yes, Doctor Murphy?" Blue eyes dancing impishly.

"Do you think you might modulate your voice in the corridors of this unit?"

"I'll try, Doctor Murphy." A quick hint of pain in the same blue eyes, enough to break your heart.

"You'll have to do better than try, Miss Ryan."

"Yes, Doctor Murphy." The imp bounced back. "Why do you talk so funny, Doctor Murphy? Are you from somewhere strange?"

"I was raised in Boston."

"Well, you're honest about it."

Much laughter from the other students.

"I don't want this program"—my face flaming—"to become a wrestling match between us, Miss Ryan."

"That might be fun."

More laughter. First point to Miss Ryan.

—*from* Happy Are Those Who Thirst for Justice

169

He strode up and down the empty streets with confident steps. It was surely a picturesque little place for Chicago, a Disneyland version of a typical affluent American neighborhood, an image not ruined by the Irish faces on hordes of children, because the children were still in school. The neighborhood was more attractive perhaps than it was when he was growing up. By returning for the reunion, he told himself, he had faced the demons from the past, exorcised them, left them behind, purged them from his life.

—from Valentine's Night

IX
The University

Many of my people are associated with the University of Chicago, or, as it is known by folks along the lakefront, *the* University (just as Beverly Country Club is called *the* Club). Roger Farrell and Sean Seamus Desmond are on the faculty, the former a member of the government department, the latter a Nobel Prize–winning biologist. Hugh Donlon earns his doctorate and loses his priesthood at the university. Chuck O'Malley graduates from the university after he has been thrown out of Notre Dame. Both Rosie Clancy and Anne O'Brien attend the school, the latter earning an M.A. in art history. Although it is not generally known, Monsignor John Blackwood Ryan presides over a seminar in the divinity school one quarter a year. One of his brothers-in-law (Nancy Ryan's husband) is a professor in the statistics department.

Nonetheless, my stories contain few descriptions of the physical appearance of the university. As I look at the photos, I realize that the campus has many beautiful sights and wonder why I had not noticed their beauty before I began to look at them through the camera lens. Perhaps the combination of the grim, gray Gothic of Ralph Adams Cramn and Chicago winters have depressed me for the quarter century I have been associated with the university community (always, truth to tell, in an ambiguous relationship). In any event, there are perspectives and vistas in the campus that are downright charming.

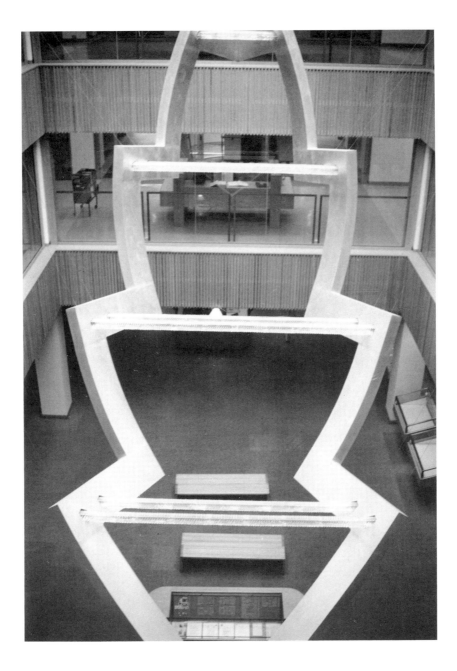

Sean Desmond is interested in angels, and he hears there is a sculpture of an angel on campus. Feckless and leprechaunish character that he is, Desmond visits the sculpture and fantasizes about it.

After lunch Sean inspected the four-story sculpture called Crystara. *This man Mooney was good, he decided, damn good. Long, graceful, rounded aluminum struts bound together by solid bars of Waterford crystal—think of how many bottles of Black Bush or Jameson's Special Reserve that much crystal might hold.*

He climbed up the stairs of the library, circling the atrium all the way to the fourth floor. At every level and from each angle at a level, Crystara *looked different, a graceful, elegant, colorful work—light yet solid, dainty yet massive, intricate yet simple, incorporeal yet preempting all the space in the atrium.*

Was it an image of an angel?

Could be, Sean decided. Why not? Could he work it into the draft he was preparing for the Royal Swedes? Maybe.

On the top floor, facing the statue, Sean concluded that, angel or not, Crystara's *shape from this perspective was definitely womanly, a woman graciously and generously opening herself up so that a man might enter her.*

What a wonderful idea for the round table tomorrow.

They might take the sculpture down if he suggested that.

—from Angel Fire

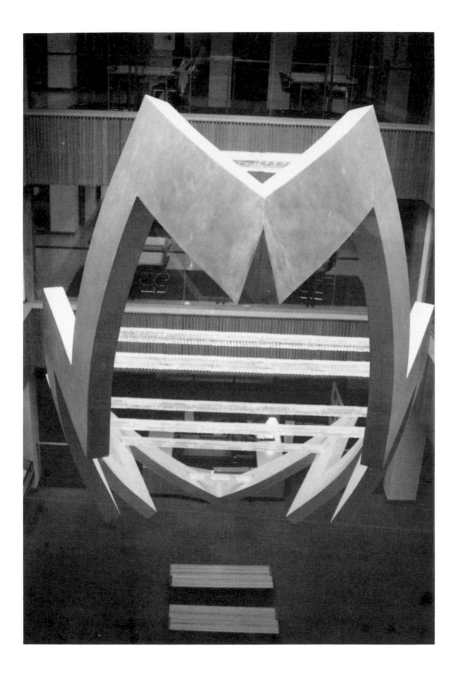

Holy Family

X
Other Neighborhoods and Their Churches

Chicago is a city of neighborhoods both because of its immigrant origins and because of its radically democratic form of city government—each alderman represents a small district, an affront to reformers who want to ignore what they take to be the prejudices of the small districts and who prize only aldermen who are as intelligent as they are.

The aldermen, reformers tell us, are inarticulate and dumb and often corrupt. Unlike reformers and activists and other such folk, however, aldermen are reelected by ordinary people.

Reformers are jealously protective of their own neighborhoods and demand that their elected representatives protect those neighborhoods.

It depends on who you are, I guess.

In any event, Chicago seems to be unalterably a city of neighborhoods and therefore a city of churches.

St. John Cantius

Notre Dame de Chicago (The French Church)

We drove south on the expressway, passing on the right the boundary of the royal borough of Bridgeport, with the impeccably neat old frame bungalows and streets so clean that it was, indeed, credible that housewives scrubbed the sidewalks every night. Then we slipped by the fringes of Englewood and Woodlawn, with their ravaged two-flats and apartment buildings, as devastated as any air-raid landscape.

We left the Dan Ryan, breaking, as it were, with the city of Chicago, passed briefly over Studs Lonigan's neighborhood and onto the battered Chicago Skyway, which carried us briefly through the aging steel mill community of Eddie Vrdolyak's tenth ward, and entered the Indiana Tollroad. The oil refinery haze of Hammond, the fires and chaste white smoke of Gary, the great black steel mills, seemed a surrealistic painting on the sky over Lake Michigan and under the implacable May sun, an intensely vital kaleidoscope of color, light, and energy.

—from Rite of Spring

Chicago's Most Famous Bungalow

Some neighborhoods have churches in double digits. Beverly had twenty-one the last time I counted, two of them Catholic. Bridgeport contains seventeen Catholic churches.

Catholics identify their origins by telling you the parish they're from—C.K. (Christ the King), Barnabas, Thomas More, Angela, Res(urrection). In some neighborhoods you can find four Catholic churches in the same two-block area—one for each nationality.

The immigrants brought their religion with them and built their churches as the center of their new communities. The Irish, ultimate pragmatists, built schools first and used the school halls for churches; the Poles theorized that the skyline of the new communities should remind the immigrants of their towns and villages in Poland, so they built the big, old-world churches that line the Kennedy Expressway.

Just as the elite of the city do not like the neighborhoods much (except their own), the archdiocese doesn't care much for the neighborhood churches (though it spends thousands to put an ugly new organ into Blackie's cathedral).

The immigrant churches—Holy Family, "the church of the prairies"; St. Mary of the Angels, the most beautiful of the Polish churches; St. George, Lithuanian; St. Martin of Tours with its golden horsemen, arguably the most beautiful church in Chicago—are marked for destruction.

St. Mary of the Angels

St. Stan's, mother parish of Chicago's Polish.

St. Patrick's

The only ethnic churches are torn down in the inner city, and "worship centers"—innocent of beauty—are constructed for the blacks and named after the community. No longer does the parish have a saint; it is merely the Catholic Community of Englewood. The poor apparently don't merit either a church or a saint.

Landmarks of the city? Landmarks of the neighborhoods? Tear them down anyway!

Holy Family is the third-oldest public building in the city, after the Water Tower and Old St. Patrick's. In the view of the Catholic Church, strapped for funds because of lay anger over the incompetence and insensitivity of church leaders, all age means is that a building is old and costly to repair.

Tear it down!

206

St. Martin of Tours

Old St. Patrick's would have met the same fate if two creative and zealous priests had not turned it into one of the most active and popular parishes in the city—proving perhaps that some residue of imagination and vitality does exist in the Catholic community.

On the Feast of All the Saints, Red Kane went to St. Patrick's for mass in honor of his dead brother. Afterward he found that, quite against his wishes, someone wanted him to become one of All the Saints. Listen to him speak about Old St. Patrick's.

So, instead of writing a column about Dav, he had gone to Mass today in memory of his brother, not sure Dav would still need prayers, not sure there was anyone to hear his prayers, and not sure that what he was doing was prayer.

The Cathedral was closer than Old St. Pat's, but he had not wanted any of the older women employees of the HG to see him at Mass. His reputation as a "fallen away" had been too carefully cultivated to be given up so easily.

He confidently expected that the Mass—or Eucharist, as his kids called it—would be lifeless and dull. The handsome young priest, however, by his own admission inspired by the solid phalanx of statues that lined either side of Old St. Pat's—"Black, Hispanic, Native American, Italian, Swedish, German even," a gesture toward Mary and Joseph, "two Jewish saints"—preached a brisk and incisive homily (the name for sermons these days) about the achievement of sanctity through generosity and kindness in everyday life—almost as if he knew that it was a memorial service for Dav. Instead of indulging in a tear or two, partly for Dav but mostly for himself, Red was forced to consider how he measured up to the criteria of the homily.

—*from* Patience of a Saint

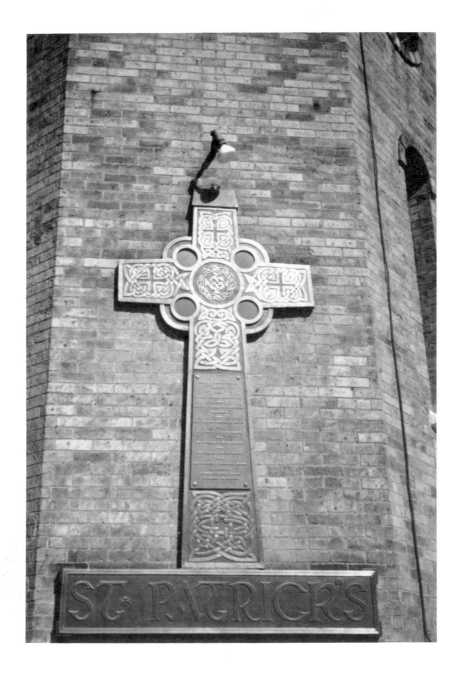

209

XI
Grand Beach

Grand Beach, it can be quite properly said, is not part of Chicago, not even if the mayor's family summers there. It's in Michigan. Indeed, heaven save us, it functions on eastern time.

Actually it doesn't. Whatever the legal time might be a mile into the state of Michigan, the villagers remain on Chicago time because, as Trish Ryan observes, all the TV programs are on Chicago time.

Indeed, the TV antenna on top of Sears Tower and the John Hancock Center can be seen from Grand Beach, thirty-five miles across the lake. So of course it *is* part of Chicago—and a warm and welcome place for the people in my stories.

Sometimes odd things happen at Grand Beach, as when the God game opens a port between our cosmos and another one, a port that happens to be centered on the beach itself. The narrator, who is not the author nor even the author behind the author, reports on how various citizens observe the change in the community when influences from the other cosmos (one "just down the street") begin to invade.

"Strange night in Grand Beach." Rich Daley withdrew his unlighted cigar and smiled the most dazzling smile in American political life.

"Restless adolescent natives?"

"Restless everyone."

"A lot of the drink taken?"

"Funny thing," the cigar back in his mouth. "Less than usual. People were sort of laid back and relaxed, like they should be at a resort, instead of uptight. It should always be that way, shouldn't it?"

"Sounds almost like a religious festival."

"Just what I thought, peaceful, and," big grin, "really sensual."

"Heaven help us all when the Grand Beach Irish turn sensual."

"Less work for my people if everyone was that way all the time."

—*from* God Game

Rev. William Henkel and friend

Our Lady of Grand Beach

Teri

"Noele"

Liz

Sir Rocco and Jennifer

Sean

Kids

223

Conor Clarke, an "old" man at twenty-eight, gets no respect from teenagers or twenty-five-year-old Diana Lyons when he goes over to Pine, not even when he demonstrates that he is better than the rest of them.

After considerable argument, protest, threats of dire punishment, recrimination, and excuses, pleas, and complaints, Con was at last persuaded to jump, clumsily, into the water. He struggled awkwardly to put on the ski. In his prime he was surely better at the sport than the others. But he was past his prime, as was evident when he fell on his face in his first try—to the hoots and hollers of his three enemies.

He managed to get out of the water the second time and promptly fell on the opposite end of his anatomy. The hoots and hollers were louder.

Finally the moves came back, he rose, rather shakily from the depths, maintained his balance for the last crucial seconds, and sped across the wake. The hoots and hollers stopped.

He was exhausted but triumphant when he climbed up the ladder into the back of the boat.

"Not bad," the Cat admitted.

"For an old man," Diana agreed, somewhat chastened. "Brute strength, but a lot of it."

"Honest, Conor," the Cat insisted, "I SAW it with my own eyes. It looked just like the Loch Ness monster!"

"Really," Conor agreed. "She was here when I was a teenager, twenty years ago."

"I thought it was longer than that."

—*from* Love Song

"The Cat"

Like all of us, the Ryans bitterly resent the end of summer and try to squeeze the last drop out of it.

Outside, under a cover of late-August stars, in which it was alleged you might find Halley's comet if you tried hard, the waters of Lake Michigan licked softly against our beach. It was the kind of warm summer night toward the end of August, to which you wanted to cling as you would to the last taste of a Sachertorte—so my wife had said earlier when we were climbing out of our pool, not yet disturbed by the late night call from her answering service.

The Ryan family's metaphors usually referred to food.

—*from* Happy Are Those Who Search for Justice

XII
O'Hare

Many of my people come home—Jim O'Neill, Neil Connor, Danny Farrell, Catherine Collins, Mike Casey. They come home, as do most of us, through O'Hare International Airport. Some are tempted to leave again, but they are not given a chance.

He saw it coming. Just as long ago, at the crack of a bat, he had been able to see a line drive headed for deep left center when he was playing the third-base line. He would begin to run as soon as the ball left the bat, knowing that he would not be able to get there in time to catch it.

Oh, yes, he saw it coming and knew that his destiny was written on it.

"Daniel Xavier Farrell," she began solemnly. "Father . . ." Her voice wavered and tears formed in the bog fire. "It's time you grew up and totally acted like an adult. You're magic, just like Moms says. She needs a magic husband and I need a magic . . ." Again the quivering lip and now the first tears spilling out of the swamp. "A magic daddy."

Done. Finished. Forever. The wandering days are over, boyo.

He linked arms with his Easter/Christmas mother/child and began to walk with her to the escalator, which would lead eventually to the parking lot of O'Hare International Airport and the rest of his life.

"Tell me about it."

—*from* Lord of the Dance